OUR FAMILY SECRET, MY MOTHER'S LIE

Our Family Secret, My Mother's Lie

A TRUE STORY ABOUT ADOPTION

John N. Reynolds

Library of Congress Control Number:		2009914286
ISBN:	Hardcover	978-1-4500-2336-8
	Softcover	978-1-4500-2335-1
	Ebook	978-1-4500-2337-5

This book was printed in the United States of America.

To order additional copies of this book, contact:
Xlibris Corporation
1-888-795-4274
www.Xlibris.com
Orders@Xlibris.com
70608

Contents

After all is said and done, you may ask, "Did you love your mother?"

The answer is, of course I did, as all children do.

What I did not like was all the secrets and lies.

That is why I dedicate this book

In loving memory to:

ZONA MAY JOHNSON

ZONA MAE HAUGHT

ZONAMAE REYNOLDS

MY MOTHER

Acknowledgments

I would like to acknowledge everyone who has encouraged me to write this story. Everyone I told it to that said this would be a good book. Thank you for the encouragement to finally write it. I want to especially thank my loving wife Juanita who kept after me to sit down and write something. She has been the force behind me to get this thing done. I love you and your support.

I wish to acknowledge Dayton and Virgi Noland who helped fill in the rest of the story and introduced me to my Ohio family. Dayton helped me do the research in the court houses of Ohio. I want to thank my cousins David, Barbara, and Joe for being there when I needed them and for their love and support. I wish to thank Naomi Morgan for all her love and encouragement and her family charts.

I want to thank a very dear friend of mine, Barbara Holloway, for telling me to move forward and just do it. Also, for helping me put this book together and making it better. I appreciate your kindness, help and support.

There are many others out there I want to thank, you all know who you are, and time and space on this page is not enough.

I want to thank all the relatives in both families for their understanding of why I had to write this book at this time. It is for other families to read and see that secrets and lies are not the best answer to some situations. This family secret, and lie, has affected my life for over 44 years.

FORWARD

Well, mom died today, Monday January 12, 2009. She was 85 years old and was married for 67 years and 9 hours. She died one day after their 67th wedding anniversary thinking that she took her family secret to the grave with her. Little did she know that I have been telling others about this story for a while now. The secret became her, and was her. It literally defined her life. She was paranoid about people finding out that she was adopted all the way to the bitter end of her life.

Little did I know, that after her death, I would finally have a beginning for my story. I never could begin to write this story because I did not know where or how to begin. Now I will begin at the end, at the end of her life. It was not a pretty ending. She was mean and cantankerous to the very end. She died of Alzheimer's and was very much out of her mind.

The family secret is that my mother was adopted. That was not a pretty word in 1923/24. In fact, it was a terrible word. She would have been teased unmercifully had anyone found out about it at school. It had a very bad stigma, even within the family. Back then relatives would look down their noses at people who were adopted and tell them to mind their own business because they were adopted. Relatives would tell the adopted one that they were poor pitiable things because they were adopted and had no real family of their own. There would be constant reminders almost every day that they did not fit in because they were adopted. That is why Mabel and Norden Haught took Zona Mae to California and tried to raise her as their own daughter with only a handful of people knowing that she was adopted. They decided that it would be the family secret and no one outside the family would know.

I guess you could say that the end of mom's life was just as tragic as the beginning of her life. She was tortured in the beginning by being thrown out into a snow storm, and she died being tortured by this insidious disease. Her life began and ended painfully. She is at rest now and in a much better place awaiting the resurrection.

I have sat down to write this story many times, and wrote it many times. I have been told to re-write this story many times. My editor, has told me to re-write this story, which I did re-write. My aunt, who is a published author herself, read my re-write and told me to re-write it again. I think I finally got the message this time and will leave out all the fluff and all the extra details and will just tell you the story.

I want to thank all the Ohio family members I have met over the years who have helped me along the way to understand all the aspects of this story. They took me to gravesites and explained the lives and histories of just exactly who these people are that are buried in those graves. Thank you for all the love and support you have shown me and our family since we re-entered your world in July, 1966. I still have trouble understanding how my mother felt meeting her sister for the first time in 1966 at the age of 43. It still brings tears to my eyes, when I look back, to see them meet, hug, kiss and cry on that July day.

I want to thank David, Barbara and Joe Smith, my cousins, who are Dorothy's children, for the support and help they have given me over the years. I am sorry that time has separated us again. Barbara is the self appointed tender of Beulah's grave. Barbara has helped me deal with this family secret over the years and helped me to meet some of the people involved. I plan to put a real marker on Grandma Beulah's grave with the proceeds of this book. Not a rock, but a headstone telling the world that Beulah McKee Johnson really did exist.

If I caused any of the family any pain or embarrassment in the writing of this book, I truly apologize. That was not my intent in writing this story. It is my mother's story and became mine when she decided to tell me when I was age 17. No one has anything to be upset about. All parties in this story were trying to do what was best for two little girls, sisters, who should NOT have been split up. It is a story of how not telling someone that he or she is adopted can have such a profound and long lasting NEGATIVE affect on that person's life. Mother was never mentally the same after she learned she was adopted.

From my point of view, watching this story unfold, Aunt Dorothy and my mother Zona Mae should never have been split up. If any two girls belonged together it was them. They were two peas in a pod and should have been raised as members of the McKee family. That of course means I would not be me. What a different life I would have had.

Chapter 1

BACKGROUND

I am 59, going on 60 in just a few days, and I am still having to live with the family secret and family lie. I have known about this lie and secret since I was 17 years old. I found out about it just a few weeks before I graduated from High School. I thought I was all finished with it, but it has remained with me all these years. Now in my senior years, my parents, the perpetrators of the lie, have moved in with me to end their days. Therefore, I now face the fact that I have to deal with it all over again.

I am a member of the sandwich generation. In my case there are no children that came home, but I had to take in my parents. My mother is 84 now and has Alzheimer's disease. My father just turned 88 and is suffering from dementia, not bad right now, but he has his days. My wife is 73 so I am the youngster in the bunch. It is a long story so sit back and relax and I will try to explain all of this to you.

My name is John Norden Reynolds. I am the only child of Sylvester and Zonamae Reynolds of Los Angeles, California. I was born on November 17, 1948 in downtown Los Angeles. I was raised in West Los Angeles on Homeside Avenue. That is near the intersection of Jefferson Blvd and LaCienega Blvd. Our corner street was Hauser Blvd. It was a nice quiet street with lots of nice people on it. The street was a dead end street with lots of sycamore and pepper trees on it. It was a true melting pot of people of all kinds and varieties.

Mom, Dad and me

I attended Marvin Avenue Elementary School, Louis Pasteur Jr. High School and Alexander Hamilton High in West L.A. I had many good friends of all different faiths, cultures and ethnicities. There was Lester Abalara, Clifford Bruce, Susan Ishii, Howard Greitzer and Hans Korfin to name just a few. I was allowed to attend Hami Hi because I was a college prep student. Dorsey High was a school for truants and delinquents at that time. Consequently, I was the kid from the wrong side of the tracks, who lived in what was called a dual district which afforded me my choice of which High School to attend.

Next door to me lived my mother's parents, Mabel and Norden Haught. They were very good people and terrific grandparents. I loved them both very much. They helped raise me and gave me many of my fundamental beliefs and the puritan work ethic. My grandfather was a Foursquare, otherwise known as a Quaker, who attended the Methodist church with my grandmother who was a United Brethren member. The Methodist Religion at that time was the religion they both felt comfortable with their beliefs. My grandfather Norden, being a Quaker, had very firm and distinct beliefs. If he disagreed with what the minister said on Sunday the minister was the first to know about it and grandpa would not go back to church for several weeks.

I was to call these people Nan and Dad because they did not want to be known as "grandma" and "grandpa". I had to call my dad "daddy" to distinguish between him and my grandfather. My parents and Nan and Dad gave me a very good childhood, it was calm, quiet, and overly protective. I had everything I wanted and that my heart desired. I remember I had a push peddle tractor that was so old and dilapidated parts would fall off when I rode it. We had to use a coat hangar to keep the "hood" on it because it was so rusted. I had a very good, brand new push peddle fire truck. I had a huge Radio Flyer red wagon that I used to ride our dog Blackie around the yard in. Blackie was our very big, old Labrador Retriever. He let me do all kinds of things to him, like bite his ear and ride on him like a donkey.

We always had animals, especially cats and dogs. We had Tippy, Blackie, Patches, Ching, for dogs. Then we had April, Boots, Rusty, Tom Thumb, Sooty, Tommy, Siam, and many more cats.

My two back yards connected with a fence between my parents and my grandparents properties. It was a Garden of Eden! We had a Santa Rosa Plum tree, a cling free yellow peach tree and a white peach tree, I think it was a Babcok, with the sweetest peaches. The yellow peach tree had juicy peaches and the juice would run down your arm and the fuzz would make your lips itch. We had a concord grape vine, an apricot tree, a lemon and orange tree with huge oranges and very tart lemons. Dad planted a garden every year and we had all kinds of vegetables from it. I was forbidden to go into that garden because I would trample the plants, pull up the carrots before their time, and Dad would go out there to smoke. Yes, another family secret. I found out he smoked when I was 14. For some years L.A. allowed residents to keep chickens in the back yards, which meant I could hunt for eggs every Sunday morning. I do remember one time Nan wringing a chicken's neck for Sunday lunch. Yuck!

We also had a passion fruit vine that ran high up on the electrical wires. I had to wait for the fruit to fall before I could eat it because the vine was so high. Mostly it was food for the birds. The plums were ruby red inside and sweet, sweet, sweet. The concord grapes grew in huge bunches and I would sit back there and eat as many as I could till my hands and tongue were purple.

My dad put up a swing in the back yard when I was about 8 years old. I loved swinging and jumping out of that old thing. When I wasn't jumping out of the swing, I was jumping off the corner of the roof to our house, or out of the old plum tree. I would scare my mother half to death. On Friday nights in the summer, my dad would bring home scrap lumber from his jobs during the week and we would go on wiener roasts down at the beach in Playa del Rey, California. That was the beach that was right at the end of the runways for L.A.X., or Los Angeles International Airport. There were round concrete fire pits on the beach that you could make a huge bond fire in. When the fire and coals were just right then you could cook your dinner and roast marshmallows. When the sun went down people would add more wood and make bonfires. Meanwhile, all the planes are taking off over your head. I always wondered where they were going. At that time planes had propellers, not jets, they came later. The water was always nice and cold and the beach was always clean. Sometimes my mother's girlfriend Ann would come down with her son Eddie and her husband Russell. If we waited to go on Saturday some of my dad's family, my aunts and uncles and cousins would come along and we would be there all day and half the night. I got some righteous sunburns when we did that.

So you see my life was quite good and wonderful all the time. My dad had a really neat job with Wilshire Tile Company. The company worked mostly in the homes of the Hollywood movie stars remodeling kitchens and bathrooms. He has quite a long list of stars he has met and in whose homes he has worked. The rule was no autographs, and do not ask for pictures. Therefore, sadly, I do not have a collection of them.

We had another connection to Hollywood right inside the family. Nan's Aunt, Bertha Miller and Uncle Keiffer, had a daughter Mildred. She married Melvin Koontz the lion tamer for MGM Studios. Melvin raised Jackie, the lion you see featured at the introduction of a MGM movie. There were actually 3 Jackies that posed for that spot. Melvin was in over 900 movies but no one ever knew him He was the stand in for all the lion scenes for Johnny Weismuller and all the other actors who played Tarzan. Whenever you see a lion or panther, or tiger in an old movie, Melvin appears in the movie somewhere. If you see a man in a lion's cage cracking a whip with his back to you that is Melvin.

Uncle Keiffer had a cabin in the mountains at a place called Blue Jay. We would go up there from time to time to enjoy the fresh air and the sweet smell of the trees. I would gather some of the largest pine cones to bring home.

My dad's mother's family were German immigrants and so I had German speaking relatives. One Aunt and Uncle lived in Big Bear, Ca. and we would spend some time with them too. I liked going to Big Bear because she was a good cook and there was a donut shop on the corner from their hosue.

It was a wonderful life. I had quite a wonderful world around me as I was growing up. I had no clue that world was a lie and would come tumbling down. I would be 17 years old and just about to graduate from Hami Hi when I find out about the family lie and secret.

Every year I would receive birthday cards and Christmas cards and gifts from "the family back east", or, from "your cousins in Ohio" as mom often said. I knew my mother came from Ohio when she was 2 years old. I knew there were relatives that lived back there and would send me things. They were all cousins of mine and I was happy with that.

One of Nan's cousins started coming out to California every year to visit on the Greyhound bus. It was "cousin" Crissie. She was very nice and we had a good time while she was around. On one of her visits she announced that she was going to move out to California, as she was getting tired of the cold weather in Ohio. She went home after that visit to pack up her belongings and come out to live by us. Unfortunately she had a heart attack and died. The family secret did not come out then because I was too busy being a kid to notice that whenever I walked into a room all talking stopped.

Nope, I had to find out about the secret just two weeks before I was to graduate High School. My mother set me down in the dinning room and began to tell me this story. She started out by saying: "Those people next door you call your grandparents, are not your real grandparents. What do you think of that?" KABOOOMB!!! Talk about your opening statement catching your interest. I was floored. Flabergasted! I was also devastated, bewildered, confused, upset, mad, angry, and many other emotions went through me like a whirlwind. Then she said: "we are going to take you back to Ohio to meet the real family, all the ones that have been sending you cards and gifts over the years. You have an Aunt and Uncle and three cousins you do not know about. Your cousins names are Barbara, David and Joe. Your Aunt's name is Dorothy and she is my sister. Your Uncle's is R.B. I am going back to see her after being away for 40 years. I do not remember her as I was a baby when we came to California. However Dorothy was three years old so she knows and remembers me." At this time my mother is 40 years old and Aunt Dorothy is 43. Forty years since they were together, and my mother had last seen her. However, it was only about 30 years for Aunt Dorothy. You will see why in a minute.

I guess this is as good a place as any to fill you in on the family secret and the lie that my mother, to this very day, perpetuates. She refuses, even in her dementia to tell anyone the truth. She has become the lie. It has taken over her life and is destroying her. She has always been very negative and hard to please. She was very controlling and overly protective. She resisted change at all cost. She could not bear the thought of being separated from Nan and Dad. She was paranoid about the secret. She would beg me not to tell the Reynolds family. Here is the story as I was told it by both my mother and Nan:

CHAPTER 2

THE STORY

The year is 1923. It is November 28th to be exact. Beulah Marie McKee Johnson is giving birth to my mother, her second child by Herman Johnson on that day in Marietta, Ohio. She has been told by Dr. Johnson, possibly related, not to have any more children because she had such a hard time delivering her daughter Dorothy three years prior. It was a bad delivery, probably just like before, and Beulah would have lived had the doctor done his job right. He left some of the afterbirth in her body and Beulah died December 21, 1923 two days shy of her 23rd birthday. Herman is devastated by Beulah's death and goes on a drunk that lasts several months.

Beulah has been disowned and rejected by the McKee's and the Johnson families since marrying Herman. Beulah is buried in potter's field and Herman has a three year old girl and a new born to take care of. This is way too much for him to handle. He just lost his lovely wife, he has two brats to take care of, he lives in the city away from the family and he stays drunk most of the time.

He is very drunk one night in February, 1924. My mother, whose name is very unusual, Zona Mae, is three months old and crying her eyes out in her crib. Herman is living in an ugly apartment building on top of Harmer Hill in Marietta, Ohio overlooking the Ohio River very far below. It is snowing a bitter snow storm that only Ohio can get that time of year. It is night and bitter cold outside. Herman is so tired of hearing Zona Mae crying and screaming that he can not take it any more and opens the door and throws her outside into the cold snow storm and she lands in a pile of snow. This causes Dorothy to go into hysterics because she is old enough to know that Zona should not be out doors in the snow. She starts to pull and kick the door and yell at her father to bring Zona back inside. Instead, he opens the door and kicks Dorothy outside too. Dorothy lands in another pile of snow. She grabs up the baby and heads for the neighbor's house and Dorothy and Zona Mae are taken to the local police station and then to the orphanage.

Let me explain to you the background of Mabel Davis, to see how she and Norden Haught come into the picture. My grandmother Nan was born Mabel E. Davis, the daughter of Sam Davis, the great-grandson of Isaiah Davis, the brother of Jefferson Davis the President of the Confederate States of America. Sam's wife, Mabel's mother, died when Mabel was still a young girl. She and her brother were adopted by the Chichester family of Parkersburg, West Virginia. Anna Chichester was a Hinton from Marietta, Ohio, which is a big name and large family in that part of Southeast Ohio. Nan was welcomed into the Hinton family and treated as a full fledged member of the family as though she were blood kin.

One of the Hinton cousins, Virgi, developed a close relationship with Nan. Both of them became telephone operators and had the big switchboards set up in their homes. Virgi lived in the country and Nan lived in the city of Marietta.

When Nan was growing up she lived across the river in Williamstown, right behind the Fenton Art Glass company. Fenton is still in business today and make beautiful hand made art glass objects. Nan would crawl under the fence at night into their pile of rejects and find treasures to bring home. Fenton Glass Co. did not set up their reject shop till many years later. Nan would tell me years later that she had had quite the collection of Fenton Glass.

One evening Mabel was sitting downstairs in the parlor while her sister Mildred was upstairs getting ready to go out on a date with a young man she had recently met. His name was Norden Haught and he was in the Army. Mabel said she looked out the window and saw him coming up the walk. She told me that she said out loud: "whoop twiddle dee dee that is the man for me." Mildred never went out on that date because Mabel opened the door and took him by the arm and the rest was history. This relationship lasted for 50 years of marriage from one date and love at first sight.

Norden and Mabel set up house on Harmar Street and Mabel became the telephone operator. It was in February of 1924 that Virgi calls Mabel to tell her of the plight of this little baby and her sister that were flung out into the snow storm. Virgi had to confess it was one of her cousins on the other side of the family, that had done this. She wanted Norden and Mabel to adopt both girls and raise them together and not split them up. Being newly weds and just getting their lives together they could not afford to adopt both girls. Virgi said that if they couldn't adopt both girls, Uncle McKee wanted to adopt Dorothy but could not adopt Zona because his wife was sick with "cancer" and could not take care of a baby at this time. Mabel and Norden talked it over and due to the fact that Norden would never be able to father children they took Zona as their only child.

Norden had been in the Army as already stated above. He was part of the forces that chased Poncho Villa back and forth across the Rio Grande and failed to capture. On his way to Fort Sam Houston in San Antonio, while riding the train from Ohio, he had a high fever. It was determined when he arrived at the Fort he had the mumps. His not being treated and the long bumpy train ride had caused them to "go down on him" and he would be sterile for life.

The McKees adopted Dorothy, they were very upset that they could not adopt Zona also. Uncle McKee knew what it was like to be left an orphan, and his heart ached that he could not take both girls. He wanted to do for Dorothy and Zona Mae what had been done for him. It is a family matter and he wanted to keep it in the family. Uncle McKee and his siblings including his sister Beulah were taken in after their father, Aaron, died a sudden and tragic death. It is recorded in the County Clerks Office as suicide. He was found hanging in his barn. Uncle McKee felt that the situation with the girls was similar by abandonment, and that it was a family matter and he wanted to keep the matter in the family.

Uncle McKee was a business man who had become a judge in the circuit court. He had political aspirations and wanted to become a member of the Ohio State government. He accomplished this when he became a member of the House of Representatives of the State of Ohio. His nephew Jum McKee was Sheriff of the same county. Consequently, Dorothy has been adopted into a very good, wealthy, strong, and well connected family.

Here is the copy of the live birth certificate with my mother's name spelled as her mother Beulah wanted it spelled. Zona May Johnson, notice the two names, first and middle and the middle having a "y" at the end. During this adoption process the "y" is dropped and an "e" emerges. Somewhere down the line the two names become one with no middle name at all.

OHIO DEPARTMENT OF HEALTH

COLUMBUS

Reg. Dist. No. 1343
Primary Reg. Dist. No. 6058

CERTIFICATE OF LIVE BIRTH

Department of Commerce — Bureau of the Census

State File No.
Registrar's No.

1. PLACE OF BIRTH:	2. USUAL RESIDENCE OF MOTHER:
(a) County Washington	(a) State Ohio
(b) Marietta Twp., Marietta, O. (City, Village, Township)	(b) County Washington
(c) Name of hospital or institution:	(c) City or village Marietta, Ohio, Rt. 1 (If outside city or village, write RURAL)
(If not in hospital or institution, give street or location)	
(d) Mother's stay before delivery:	(d) Street No.
In hospital or institution _____ In this community _____ (Specify whether years, months, or days)	(If rural, give location)

3. FULL NAME OF CHILD	ZONA MAY JOHNSON	4. DATE OF BIRTH Nov. 28, 1923 (Month) (Day) (Year)

5. Sex: Female	6. Twin _____ Triplet _____	If so—born 1st, 2d, or 3d	7. Number months of pregnancy 9	7a. Weight at birth	7b. Congenital Malformation	8. Is mother married? Yes

FATHER OF CHILD	MOTHER OF CHILD
9. Full name Herman Dewey Johnson	15. Full maiden name Beulah Marie McKee
10. Color or race White 11. Age at time of this birth 25 yrs.	16. Color or race White 17. Age at time of this birth 23 yrs.
12. Birthplace Ohio (City, town, or county) (State or foreign country)	18. Birthplace Ohio (City, town, or county) (State or foreign country)
13. Usual occupation Farmer	19. Usual occupation Housewife
14. Industry or business	20. Industry or business

21. Children born to this mother not including this child 1	22. Mother's usual mailing address:
(a) How many other children of this mother are now living? 1	Marietta, Ohio, Rt. 1
(b) How many other children were born alive but are now dead? 0	
(c) How many children were born dead? 0 (The total of a-b-c should equal Item 21)	Do not write in this space

23. I hereby certify that I attended the birth of this child who was born alive at the hour of 10:15P. M on the date above stated and that the information given was furnished by. _____ related to this child as

24. Date received by local registrar 12-4-23	Signature I. J. Johnson, M. D. (Specify if physician, licensed midwife or other)
25. Registrar's signature J. Harry McClure	Address Marietta, Ohio
26. Date on which given name added _____ By _____ (Title)	Date signed _____

Later in the story I will tell you how my mother came to be in possession of these papers. I do not think she has Nan and Dad's copy, although I may be wrong about that. You decide after you read on. Now let us return to our happy families in Ohio. Mabel and Norden are very happy with Zona Mae and are getting used to having a baby around. Dad is working in a chair manufacturing company and Nan is still a switchboard operator as is Virgi.

The year is now 1926. Dorothy is 5 and Zona is 2. The adoption was final in September of 1924, so Zona has been with the Haughts for 1 year and 3 months. They have bonded and formed a family and are very happy together.

The McKees are happy with Dorothy and everything is going their way. The judge, Uncle McKee, becomes the state representative and life is very, very good. It is so good that Mrs. McKee has been given good news that her cancer is gone and she is cured and going to live a lot longer. Well now, that is a horse of a different color. The reason why they could not adopt Zona is now gone. Mrs. McKee no longer has cancer and is able to care for a baby after all. She starts to discuss with her husband just how they can go about adopting Zona Mae and reunite the two girls.

They try the direct approach by asking the Haughts if they would consider letting Zona be readopted by them. The Haughts, who have grown attached to Zona are appalled and flatly reject the offer. They said they will not give up their new daughter because they have already bonded and Mabel has nursed her through some illness she had when they got her. Mabel would always say: "The nerve of them even to ask that question." Then Mabel and Norden start to become nervous. Nan fears the worst because of the position the McKee's occupy and the power they wield. They have the ability to undo the adoption and come and take little Zona away from them. Mabel is worried sick.

Zona May and Dorothy, the last picture taken together

Uncle McKee with Zona May Johnson before she was adopted by the Haughts

Mabel has always been in contact with her Aunt in California. Mabel writes to Auntie and tells her all about the new situation and that she is scared that something will happen and Zona will be taken away. Auntie tells them not to worry and if they wish to come to California Uncle Keiffer and her will pay for their train tickets and will help them get established in California. Just let them know if they need the money for the train tickets.

Virgi, the telephone operator and cousin of Mabel, begins to overhear telephone conversations to the effect that the McKees want Zona to be with them and be reunited with Dorothy, Zona's sister. She warns Mabel that something is afoot and that they should prepare to leave for California. Mabel contacts Auntie and tells her they need the money for the train tickets. The money is sent right away by Western Union. The tickets are purchased.

Meanwhile the judge/State Rep McKee is getting a judge to nullify the adoption of Zona. He is getting a court order to take Zona away from the Haughts. Virgi is able to learn of this because she has to listen in on conversations to know when to pull the plug and release the line. She calls Uncle McKee and tells him that she has heard that the Haughts are scheduled to leave from the Marietta, Ohio depot and she gives him the date and time. Uncle McKee and his nephew the Sheriff, race down from Caldwell and go to the train station to get Zona before it is too late. However, the Haughts in fact had already boarded an earlier train at a whistle stop down the line at Constitution Hill. They left with only two suitcases of their clothes and other important things, like adoption papers. Mabel must leave behind most of her Fenton Glass collection.

Nan told me that was the longest and worst trip of her entire life. She hated crossing water and was terrified the whole time their car was on a barge crossing over the Mississippi River to get to St. Louis. She was very glad when they arrived in Los Angeles at the LaGrande Station. She was glad to be far, far away from Ohio and those people who could take their only daughter away.

I am happy to report that Herman Johnson, the grandpa I never knew or met, was able to turn his life around after meeting his second wife and together they had 7 children who would be my mother's half brothers and sisters. She was able to meet some of them during her life, but not all of them.

Auntie Bertha and Uncle Keifer kept their word and helped Nan and Norden start their new life in California. Nan and Norden stayed in a little place behind their house until Norden could find work. Norden finally got a real good job as a custodian with the Los Angeles City School System. He remained in that position for 35 years.

The Haughts would move around a few times in the L.A. area before finally finding a nice house on Adair Street. This street is about two blocks long and the cross street is Santa Barbara Avenue. To this day my mom and dad can tell you the names of everyone that lived on those two blocks. The Hawkins family, the Stertzenbaums, the Hemstreets, and of course the Reynolds family.

I do not know how old Zona was when they moved onto Adair Street but she was living there in 1936 when she was 13 years old. Those teenage years are so tender and strange with all those hormones beginning to take over. 13 is an awkward and gawky stage of life and one is usually self conscious and insecure at best at that time of life. It is not the time to find out you are adopted. Yet, that is to be Zona's fate. She will experience her whole world collapsing at the tender age of 13. In just about the time it takes to write this sentence.

Zona Mae and Norden Haught.
Do you see another family secret in this picture?

CHAPTER 3

ZONA MAE FINDS OUT
THE FAMILY SECRET

It is a beautiful, hot summer day in June or July of 1936 on Adair Street. Zona goes outside to play with her girlfriends, probably the Stertzenbaums. They are playing hop scotch and jump rope and games like these. Nan is indoors and suddenly she shivers and decides she better look outside to see if Zona is alright. She steps out on the front porch and looks up and down the street and sees Zona playing in the yard, she also sees a big car coming down the street very, very slow as if looking for an address. She sees the front license plate: OHIO. She runs out on the lawn, grabs Zona kicking and screaming off the lawn and drags her bodily into the house. She shuts the door, locks it and pulls down the door shade, closes all the curtains and is yelling for Zona to sit down and be very quiet. Zona is in shock now because she does not know what is making her mother act like a mad wild woman. She never heard Nan yell at her before. Now Nan is yelling and screaming for her to sit and be quiet. She now has to tell her about being adopted because the McKees are coming down the street in a brand new car. She tells Zona that she is adopted. They are not her real parents. She has a sister named Dorothy and she is in the back seat of that car that is now parked outside their front door. They sit and wait for the knock on the front door. They wait. They wait. They wait. No knock ever comes. You see the McKees realize by the fuss and commotion they just witnessed that Zona did not know she was adopted and that Nan was still afraid of them. They did not stop but turned around and left, and went back to Ohio. The cat is now out of the proverbial bag and the beans have been spilled.

Mother runs out of the back door and down an alley. She runs and runs and runs crying all the way. She gets to the end of the alley and stops. Here she says she "saw the most beautiful angel in all of the world." The angel tells her to stop running away, to turn around and go home to the people who love her. The angel tells her she will be alright and that they love her very, very much and all will be well. Zona turns around and walks home, sobbing.

Zona Mae age 13, the year she found out she was adopted

Meanwhile, Norden is still at work. He knows nothing of what is happening back home at his house. He will find out when he gets there. What a terrible scene he must have walked into that day. Life was forever changed for everyone on that day, but I don't think he ever recovered from that experience. He was a very quiet man, reserved and somewhat emotionally detached. I never really saw him mad but one time. That time was the day before he died and we had had an argument over my nickname, "Nordie." Nordie is a corruption of his first name Norden. He said I didn't like him or his name since I wanted to be known as John from now on. It was not that at all. I was becoming a man and I wanted to be known by my own name, John. I was not to have the chance to apologize.

The crazy part of this is that Dorothy, who already knew she was adopted and that Zona was her sister, only got a glimpse of a girl being dragged into a house in Los Angeles in 1936. She would have to wait 30 more years to finally meet her baby sister face to face.

It is on this day that the family secret is born out in California. Nan and Dad still did not want anyone to know that Zona was adopted. She was their little girl, their only child. They were so afraid someone would find out and try to take her away from them. Also, the stigma of being adopted was still a potential threat they wished to protect little Zona from. Zona was sworn to secrecy and eventually so was my dad. When my dad proposed and was to marry Zona he was told the secret by Nan and Dad and told that the Reynolds family was never to know about this. These two families did not like each other very much and did not get along well. The family secret was safe. My mother is now living a lie and knows it. The lie goes on down to this day. She denies that she is adopted. The lie is now part of her, it is her, it defines her.

In 1946 my mother receives a strange letter in the mail from an attorney in Ohio. It is a letter telling her she has an inheritance due her in the amount of $270. The letter is addressed to Mrs. Zona Johnson Haught Reynolds. It is a good thing she had found out about the Johnson part 10 years earlier. The letter is from the judge who presided over her adoption, A.A. Schramm. He had $540 that had to be split between Dorothy and Zona Mae. To this day I do not have an explanation as to the source of this money and how Mr. Schramm came to be in possession of it in a bank's savings account.

The Haught family

CHAPTER 4

I INHERIT THE FAMILY SECRET

The lie/secret is kept all the way down to my time. As already mentioned above my mother told me her story when I was about to graduate from Hamilton High. The happiest time of my life was also the most confusing time. My mother was surprised to learn that I still loved my grandparents, Nan and Dad, even more because they stepped up and adopted my mother. I was not mad at them nor did I hate them. She was upset about this, she could not understand why I did not feel the same way about "those people next door" as she did. If anything negative was felt by me at this time, it was that I was mad at her for not telling me sooner. I was mad at her for doing to me at age 17 what happened to her at age 13. She destroyed the happiest day of my life, High School Graduation. My friend Howard just told me recently that he knew something major had happened to me just before we graduated from Hami Hi but he didn't know what it was.

When we went back to Ohio that July, 1966 I was still shocked to be meeting everyone. I was very shocked to meet my Aunt Dorothy and Uncle R.B. I will never forget that day. We had driven in our brand new 1966 Chevy II station wagon over 2000 miles to Ohio. When we got to Marietta we met The Morgans, whom we stayed with, and they took us around the town to meet Aunt Junie, Aunt Ruby, cousins Virgi and her husband Dayton Noland. We went to the Hinton Family Reunion at Cutler Chapel at Constitution Hill and saw the spot where the Haughts and Zona boarded the train for California. We met Ben and Ethel Pinkerton and my grandmother's best friend Bessie Sprague. I met a whole bunch of cousins around my age and had to answer all these questions about L.A. and Hollywood and the movie stars. I was bored out of my mind. I wish I had taken along a tape recorder and recorded some of the conversations I was now able to listen to. I am sure they would have made this book a little more interesting. We never went to see Grandpa Herman Johnson who was still alive in 1966. He asked about us and wanted to see us and to meet me. Mother was livid that he even had the nerve to ask. We did not go. I should have when I went back the next year.

Dorothy and Zonamae reunited in 1966 after 38 years

Mother met some of her half brothers and sisters and allowed that they were part of her family. She remained friendly but distant. The lie was too much a part of her to let go and totally accept her real family. It was so ingrained by now that in 1970 when mother paid the airfare for her sister Dorothy and the three kids out to Los Angeles, she introduced them to everyone as her cousins. I told a few people that Dorothy was really her sister, but they chose to believe the lie and not me, after all I was a teenager and being disrespectful to my mother. So the lie continued.

As I just mentioned above, I returned to Ohio the next year, 1967, alone to stay with the family and try and get a family feeling from my relatives in Ohio. I flew to Chicago, which was my first plane trip, then from Chicago I flew to Columbus, Ohio where I boarded a bus to Caldwell. This is the year 1967. I was the big city kid coming to the country. I had longer hair, continental pants, polyester shirt, and ugly shoes. My suitcase had decals pasted all over it from every place I had ever visited. Places like Catalina, San Fransisco, San Diego, L.A. Zoo, San Diego Zoo, Disneyland and places like that. I had thick black framed glasses on and I must have looked like the Nerd who came to Ohio. I was not ready for the greeting I was to receive. You see my cousins David and Barbara had told everyone they knew that we were related to that I was coming in on the next bus. When I arrived I felt like a movie star, all these girls in sweaters and plaid skirts with hair high on their heads and well hairsprayed screaming at me. They wanted my autograph and to tell me who they were and how we were related. I was so overwhelmed I was rude to them and told them to please all go away and leave me alone, I was just another cousin coming to visit. So young, and so dumb, I should have stood there and forced myself to get their names and addresses and who they were and how we were related. It sure would have made life easier and maybe I could have found out some more information about the family that I still don't know today.

Down to this day, even with Alzheimer's Disease, mom insists she is the only child of Mabel and Norden Haught. She insists she was never adopted and that she has no other family, no brothers or sisters. She is 84 and will be 85 in November.

Apparently though in 1967, the year after our first trip back east to visit the family, curiosity got the better of her. Now that I am able to go through their personal papers and things I have found correspondence with the Health Department of Washington County Ohio concerning her adoption. She wrote two inquiries about her adoption. The second letter confirmed she had been born a Johnson and that she was in fact adopted by the Haughts in September, 1924. Now she had her own proof.

JOURNAL ENTRY -- COPY OF ORDERS. ADOPTION.

By Husband and Wife.

Probate Court, Washington County, Ohio.

September 29, 1924.

In the Matter of   /

Adoption.
Orders.

Zona Mae Johnson.   / ~~‾‾‾‾‾‾‾‾‾‾‾‾‾‾‾~~

This day this cause came on to be heard and Norden Haught and
Mabel Haught, husband and wife, having heretofore appeared in open
Court, and filed herein their petition for leave to adopt, and change
the name of Zona Mae Johnson, child of Herman D. Johnson, the mother
being dead; with the answer and consent in writing of Herman D.
Johnson, father of said Zona Mae Johnson.

And the Court being fully advised in the premises, finds that
said petitioners are residents of #220 Harmar Street, Marietta, Ohio,
Washington County, and that said Zona Mae Johnson is of the age of
3 months, on the 28th day of ~~November 1923, and resides in Washington~~
County, Ohio, and that the said Mabel Haught wife and Norden Haught
husband were examined separate from each other, from which examination
the Court is satisfied that said husband and wife, each of their own
free will and accord, desire such adoption; and the Court being satisfied of the ability and fitness of the petitioners to bring up and
educate such child properly, having reference to the degree and condi-
tion of the child's parents, and that said adoption is fit and proper.

It is therefore considered and ordered by the Court, that from the
date of this order the said Zona Mae Johnson be and is, to all legal
intents and purposes, the child of said petitioners Norden Haught and
Mabel Haught, and that the name of said child be and is hereby changed
from Zona Mae Johnson, to Zona Mae Haught.

I, ...A.A.Schramm..Judge and Ex-Officio

Clerk of the Probate Court, within and for said County, having the custody of the FILES, JOUR-

NALS AND RECORDS of said Court, do hereby certify that the foregoing is a true copy of........

the entry spread upon the Journal of this Court, relative to the...

Adoption and changing of name, of Zona Mae Johnson................

....

....

....

....

as the same appear............upon the...Journal..........of said Court, and I further Certify

that I have carefully compared the foregoing copy with the original on....Journal................

....and that the same is a full and correct transcript thereof.

IN WITNESS WHEREOF, I have hereunto set my hand and affixed the seal of said Court, at MA-

RIETTA, O., this..2nd....day of......October............A. D. 19 24.

A.A.Schramm

Probate Judge and Ex-Officio of said Court.

By *Ethel M. Ward* Deputy Clerk.

It would be another 30 years, 1997, before I would try and unravel the information about my mother's adoption. I would be 50 years old and still wondering about it all and if I could get my hands on some of the documents. That was the year that we took our Fall vacation and ended up in Ohio doing my research.

CHAPTER 5

THE FINAL FALL SEARCH

I went to the court house of Washington County and began to inquire about adoptions in the year 1924. Of course the formal answer is that they are sealed and no one is allowed to view them. I was told it would take a lawyer and a court order to get them so that I could read them. One of the clerks heard me ask about the date and she took me aside and asked if I knew a more specific date. I told her it had to be around February, 1924. She pointed to a large folio book case and told me to look on the third shelf for the year 1924. It is the records of the court reporter which are a part of public domain and therefore not sealed, it is public record. I found the book of the transcripts of the court proceedings and glanced over them till I saw the name Zona Mae Johnston in the February file. The transcribed notes from shorthand gave me all that I needed to know about the details surrounding my mother's adoption. I could not copy them, so I made a hand written copy.

General Docket #H pg 237

In the Matter of
the adoption of
Zona Mae Johnston
by
Norden Haught
&
Mabel Haught

Used & cause cont'd
for 6 mos
Sept 29, 1924
Final Orders
& adoption
entered

Adoption
Feb 18, 1924 —
petition for
Adoption of
Zona Mae Johnston
by Norden Haught
& Mabel Haught
filed; also answer
of consent of
father filed
Cause continued
Mar 1 1924 consent
of Herman Johnston
father of said child
filed
Mar 1, 1924 hearing

I was amazed at all the things I could get from all the clerks of court in the small courthouses we visited. I have wills, birth certificates, death certificates, marriage information, and lots of personal information on many of the McKees and want to go back and get more on the Johnson family. I really would like to solve the problem of why my grandmother Beulah is buried outside the cemetery and next to the plot of her grandmother and why no one claimed her body and wanted to give her a proper burial. This is still a puzzle I will probably never solve, or did not listen to the answer in 1966 when it was being discussed and I was being so bored.

It was easy to catch the genealogy bug. My wife and I had so much fun doing this together. We marched up and down the hills of Ohio going from cemetery to cemetery looking for McKee and Johnson graves and headstones. The best one we found was for a dentist from County Down, Ireland. So I am able to gather that my mother's family hails from County Down Ireland.

A very unusual thing happened to us as we were gathering our information on Beulah McKee Johnson. We were told at the Court House in Marietta about the mortuary that probably handled her funeral. They would have some records we would be interested in. So around the corner we went to the mortuary, the oldest in town. It was rather an old eerie place, very dark and dank and had the old sconce lamps along the walls of the center hall that was lined with very dark wood work. The light bulbs had to be 20 watt bulbs. It was so dark your eyes had to adjust before you could proceed down the hallway. We go to the desk and this old man, rubbing his hands together and moving like a bird of prey came hoping over to us and asked if he could be of any service to us. Chills ran down my spine. A second later his wife, just as old and hobbling, rubbing her hands together asked if we needed any of their services. Another chill ran down my spine and my hair prickled at the back of my neck. No we said we just needed some information on my grandmother. She asked who that would be and I told her Beulah McKee Johnson. "Oh my, what took you so long to come, we have been looking for someone of her relatives to come for so long. We are so glad you finally came. Just a minute I have the book right over here." She took down an old book from a shelf that contained information from past funerals and blew off the dust. She turned to a marked place in the book and low and behold there was Beulah's name and all her statistics. "We knew someone would finally come to make this right someday. We are so glad to meet you."

You see what they were talking about is the fact that neither family would claim Beulah's body for burial. Finally, Beulah's maternal grandmother allowed Beulah to be buried outside the family plot and OUTSIDE THE FENCE of the cemetery. Their plot bordered the fence, and Beulah is outside the fence alongside her grandmother's grave. All these years a rock has marked the spot. When Barbara and I were there the rock had moved and when Barbara paid to have the grave probed there was nothing there. I had to explain that the grave had to be higher and next to her grandmother's grave. Barbara was horrified to find out we were related to "those people" because for years there was "bad blood between the two families."

CHAPTER 6

AFTERWORD

I am fascinated at all the lives this secret has touched, in good and bad ways. It has had an affect on all of us and has effected all of us greatly. It starts with Herman Johnson losing his wife in childbirth. The two little girls, Zona Mae and Dorothy who are so cruelly thrown outside in a winter snow storm, are the ones directly affected by this adoption. Dorothy has to live with the memory of that night, that Zona was too young to remember. Virgi wanted to beat her cousin Herman to a pulp when she found out what he did, but tried her best to salvage a bad situation. The McKee's tried to do their best and circumstances kept them from taking both girls. The Haught's were newly weds and could only afford to take one child.

This is a tragedy that the girls were split up and it would take 40 years for them to reunite. The biggest tragedy, that could have been avoided is Zona not knowing until she was 13 years old, and her family shows up at the front door. Mother should have known all along that she had a sister back in Ohio. It was a cruel way to find out that she was not the blood related daughter of the Haughts. The McKees could have written to tell Mabel they were coming out to visit, but when you want to surprise someone you usually do not announce it.

Zonamae is the tragedy here. She becomes unstable all of her life. Friends are now telling me that she had problems from then on in school, and with people. She began to cling to Mabel and Norden. Nan once told me that they rented a house for my mom and dad about 5 miles away so they could have some space. Zona would have none of it and cried hysterically until they could come back home. Mom's life was changed forever and she lived a lie and in denial every step of the way, every single day, down to this very day. Mother was very controlling, opinionated and resisted change at every turn. She ruled over my father and me until I was able to leave and get away from home. When she had to come live with my wife and me she tried to rule over us all over again but we would not allow it.

Nan and Dad Haught were very affected by all of this. Poor Dad had to come home and walk into the middle of this tragedy, his life and theirs, changed from then on. Yet they chose to continue the lie and keep the secret. That is a huge tragedy but must be understood in the light of the 1920's and 1930's. It was a huge stigma in society to have been an adopted child. It was even worse for the ones that had to adopt and could not have their own children. People would gossip about this and looked down upon adopted ones and it played a part of your status in the community. It was a black mark on you and you would be looked at as abnormal. The life Nan and Dad tried to protect Zona from would become a reality in a new location. Instead of it happening in Ohio it would take place in Los Angeles, a much bigger arena. Mother would have been poked fun at, ridiculed, called names and teased unmercifully. They had to keep it a secret, or move away again and start all over.

My father came into the secret when he married into the family. He kept it faithfully too. Why they wanted me to know it is a puzzle. They could have kept it a secret until now and I would not have known about it until I was 60 years old. I have all the papers in my possession now and know more now than I did back then.

I must admit that I have not kept this a secret from everyone. I have told several aunts and uncles over the years and my cousin Kari knows and has for a long time. I did not see the big deal because by the 1960's there was no stigma on adoption. It was a good thing to be adopted and you were no longer looked down upon and the black mark was removed.

I have had to struggle with this secret because I had the normal reaction that my mother should have had when she was 13 and found out about it. Instead it was left up to me. I want to know everything there is to know. I want to know all my relatives that were hidden from me and who they are and all about them. I should have gone to see my Grandpa Herman when I went back alone. I did not have the nerve to see him and wanted to respect my mother's wishes. That is a cop out, I was afraid to meet him. That was stupid. Now all I have is a picture of him and a deep curiosity about him. I really should have moved back to Ohio for a couple of years to meet everyone and get to know them better.

If I had done that I would have been able to put in a claim for my mother's inheritance of the Johnson Family farm. The year my wife and I went up there we found out it was too late because the farm had been sold out of the family the year before. Always a day late and a dollar short, however, I was never after any kind of inheritance. It is interesting to note that when a long lost relative suddenly shows up people become suspicious of your intent. I was not looking for any inheritance, instead, I was looking to understand all that had gone on before me and to search for things my mother did not want to know. I would have been able to really know these people better. My life would surely have been different. Ah, we grow too soon old and too late smart. That is a German expression.

My mother and Aunt Dorothy did receive some kind of an inheritance, albeit a small one, from some attorney when he died. It was a strange amount and no reason was given for it. Since everyone is now dead there is no finding out what it was and from whom it came.

Apparently there are still secrets and lies that I do not know about and may never know. Some are small, and none so far as big as this one. I must say this secret of theirs has sent me in different directions at different times of my life. It has been a part of my life. I have not been able to stop thinking about it, for it is there every day. For example, one winter Aunt Dorothy asked me to come see her for the last time as she was dieing of breast cancer. I packed up the car, kissed the wife goodbye and headed up to Ohio from Louisiana. I was not really thinking about any thing much and was in a good mood until I got to Charleston, West Virginia. This feeling of home, family, history, melancholy, sadness and deep depression came over me. I became happy, sad, confused, with a feeling that I was coming back home. Now I was born in Los Angeles, I was not coming back home. Was I having my mother's feelings for her? I had this very big feeling of being home and having been away for a very long time. It was so over powering I had to stop at a rest area to gather myself.

I guess most of the people are now dead that this has had any personal bearing on. I am writing this for my own understanding and catharsis and not to hurt any more people and their feelings. Enough of that has gone on now for 85 years. I am trying to put all of this into perspective and look at it from the standpoint of what it must have been like in the 1920's and 30's when all of this was going on. I think it is a fascinating story and picture of how adoption affects so many people. It has ripples that pass through time. It is not just about the family who gives a person up for adoption, or is it about the person who is given up for adoption. No, it is many more people and even transcends time. Adoption must not be kept as a dirty secret, never to be mentioned. The adopted child should know from the very beginning that they are adopted and loved very much.

CHAPTER 7

IN CONCLUSION

Adoption is a wonderful choice and should be celebrated. It should not be a difficult task to know your past and find out about it. I was able to learn, through a back door, all I needed to know from the transcriptions of the clerk of court. It causes too much pain for the adopted ones to go through to find out the information that is rightfully theirs. It is their past, their family, their heritage. It is needed to be known so that a brother and sister, separated at birth but brought up in the same community with the adoptions kept secret, do not fall in love and marry and try to have children. This leads the mind to boggle over the possibilities that could come from this. It is a moral dilemma also.

Every adopted child should know that they were adopted because they have the right to find out who they are and where they come from. Mothers and Fathers have the right to privacy when giving up a child for adoption. They should have a box that says "do not wish to be found". That would tell the adopted child they do not wish to meet face to face in the future. However, all of the vital information including their names should be given to the adopted child when they request them. The pain that would come from realizing they do not wish to meet can be dealt with at that time. It is a lesser pain than knowing but never being able to find out anything.

This opens a door for more moral questions. It creates dilemmas of several kinds down the road. That is for another person to write a different book about. It is enough to think about my mother's and my pain.

I must say that along the way I have met some very nice family members. I could not have written this story without the help and encouragement of Dayton and Virgi Noland, Naomi Morgan, and other members I met along the way. Virgi helped fill in some of the details from her point of view and part of the story. I met some of the major players of this story over the years and have found them to be very nice and very good people. I do have good family members from my mother's side of the family. I am happy that they were not hidden from me forever.

For example, while standing in an ice cream shop in the square in Caldwell, Ohio in 1997 I met a very nice family member. I was going through a box of old photos of the town of Caldwell. What caught my eye was a bunch of pictures with steam locomotives in town at the depot. I mumble sometimes out loud and was wondering if any of these good people in these pictures were family members. The proprietor of the store heard me and asked what family names I was looking for and if I was from there. Well, the story started to come out about mom and the adoption and the family names of my relatives and her mouth flew open. It seems I was talking to one of my cousins. She made us come to her house to fill out the family tree book she had. When she opened it up to my page she had my name and nothing else. We sat and talked about how she knew of me and now had the opportunity to fill in the rest of my history. I met her son and found out we have so much in common. We both love the Civil War period of our nation's history and we both love trains.

I must admit it has been an unusual journey over the years, especially all the trips to all the family gravesites in all the many cemeteries on the hillsides of Ohio. It seems that every time I have sat down to work on this, or go to Ohio to find out more information, it has been in the autumn. How fitting that this book should come out in the autumn and the autumn of my life. Now I am looking back at the story from a 60 year old man's perspective. I could never imagine how this would end and what kind of ending I would have for this book.

Now that my parents have come to live with me, I have learned even more secrets. It seems that Dad was in love with a beautiful black woman back in 1939 and even asked her to marry him. She accepted and her family welcomed my Dad. Her father was a doctor and her mother was a nurse. However, when Grandma Reynolds found out about it she put an end to it. My mother was second choice while dad was on the rebound.

Another more shocking secret is that Dad showed me the divorce papers he had drawn up in the Army. He had just made Sergeant when he found out that mother was not faithful to him. He had the other man's name, place of birth, branch of the armed services, and rank. He was going to divorce mother but found out if he did that while still in the Army, he would lose everything, pension, rank, and any hope of future advancement. So he did not proceed with the divorce. He chose to forgive mother. I had the golden opportunity to read the entire thing when dad brought the WWII letters here with him. But one morning I woke up to a trash can full of shredded WWII letters. He said that those things were past and forgotten. He also said they were between him and mother only and no one else. I can respect that. I just wish, from a family historian point of view, that I could have read them to get the real feel for the rest of the story. You see he knows I am writing this book.

All things considered it is a miracle that I am here. I am so glad I am here and that I have had this opportunity to show a glimpse of how families work. They try to protect their own by adopting to keep family together. Technically Mabel and Norden were family too, albeit shirt tail relatives, and by adoption no less. I tried to show that keeping a secret like this one can cause irreparable harm when the secret comes out. The old line that "the truth will out" is one thing you can count on. It will come out accidentally or on purpose, but it WILL COME OUT, and usually not in a very pretty way.

There should be no shame or guilt to being adopted. It is also a testament to the fact that families should not be split up. The families that are involved in this "secret" were both acting out of love. Love for two little girls that were part of "the family". Nan was a very distant "relative" and only part of the family by being adopted herself by the Chichesters. I really want this secret to go away. It will when all of us are dead and gone. By now let us hope that all wounds have healed. We cannot undo the past. We can forgive and forget and move forward. That is why I wrote this book. However, if the family secret had not worked out this way I would not be me, I would not be sitting here writing all of this down. I must say I would not even be alive if it weren't for Our Family Secret, My Mother's Lie.

While preparing to put this book together and published, after my mother's death, I came across old photographs I did not know my mother had. She has pictures of herself as a 3 or 4 month old baby being held by Uncle McKee as you have already seen in this book. It was taken the same day as the picture of her and Dorothy together. I had no idea what he looked like, and now have a picture of him holding my mother. The adoption was finalized when mother was 9 months old and she went to live with the Haughts. She was two years old when they left in a rush for Los Angeles.

It is obvious that these pictures are surfacing that there was communication between Zonamae and Dorothy after the 1935 fiasco. Relatives sent pictures of themselves and other relatives and on the back they say: "give this one to Zona Mae, she can have it", or, "Zona Mae this is so and so your aunt and her children." Dorothy even sent pictures of herself and Uncle R.B. along with David, Barbara and Joe as young children. So pictures were sent along with letters before the 1966 meeting.

It seems that Grandma Chichester, Mabel's adopted mother, sent a lot of photos of herself and Grandpa Chichester and many other relatives. There are some of Aunt Alice, Aunt Bina, Aunt Budda and other relatives such as cousins. It is nice to know that these relatives stepped up to help mother know her Ohio family once they knew that Zonamae knew "the secret". They wanted her to know her family and have pictures and names to go with them. This was an outreach of love on their part.

When we arrived in Ohio, it was Herman and Naomi Morgan that helped show us through genealogy pages how it all fit together. In addition, Dayton Nolan had written a book of family history, mostly his and Virgi's, but about some of the relatives that he was able to research. For example, he found a cousin in the Civil War that kept switching sides and fighting for the side that captured him.

It seems that every family has its self-appointed historian. I am mine. I still have to do the Reynolds family clan, including the Zastrows, the German side of my father's family. I also need to do the Johnson family. I need to live two more life times to get it all done. It took 60 years for this one. It is the most rewarding experience I have ever had. It is an emotional roller coaster to say the least, but a ride that is well worth it. To know who you are and where you come from is the most valuable information anyone can have.